Christmas Cookies

'Tis the Season!

Contents

Fundamentals

4 The Four Basic Formulas

➤ 5 **Troubleshooting**

6 Tools

➤ 7 **Decorating Made Easy**

8 The ABC's of Ingredients

Recipes

10 Cookie Dough—Endlessly Versatile

30 Cookie Batter—Sometimes Twirled, Sometimes Spread Flat

42 German Gingersnap (Lebkuchen) Dough—A Taste of Christmas!

52 Macaroon Batter—Delicate Seduction

Appendix

60 Index
62 Credits
64 **10 Tips for Success:
Guaranteed Perfect
Christmas Cookies**

Cookie Favorites

Each year before the Christmas holidays, we haul out the cookie cutters, roll up our sleeves, and dive into baking. And what better way to awaken the Christmas spirit than to fill the house with the wonderful aroma of cookies? This little book presents both classics and new cookie recipes, all of them certain to put you in a baking mood!

The Four Basic Formulas

Cookie Dough

Makes 48 cookies
2 cups flour
$2/3$ cup sugar
$1/2$ cup softened butter
1 egg

In a bowl, knead all the ingredients together and form smooth dough.

Secrets to success: After kneading, wrap the dough in plastic wrap and refrigerate for 1 hour. On a floured work surface, roll out the dough to the thickness of the back of a knife blade and cut out the cookies. Line a baking sheet with parchment paper and transfer the cookies to a baking sheet.

Cookie Batter

Makes 48 cookies
1 cup softened butter
$1/3$ cup powdered sugar
$1/2$ tsp vanilla extract
2 eggs
$1 1/4$ cups flour
1 tsp baking powder
2 cups ground hazelnuts

Cream together the butter and sugar. Stir in eggs, followed by flour, baking powder, and nuts.

Secrets to success: Place the batter in a pastry bag with a star tip and pipe it onto a baking sheet lined with parchment paper. Put stiff batters through a cookie press.

German Gingersnap (Lebkuchen) Dough

Makes 1 sheet
$3/4$ cup honey
$1/2$ cup sugar
$1/4$ cup butter
$2 1/3$ cups flour
1 tsp baking powder
$1/4$ cup chopped candied orange peel
1 egg
2 tsp Lebkuchen spice (specialty food market, or mix equal parts of dried bitter orange peel, dried lemon peel, cinnamon, cloves, star anise, ginger, nutmeg, and cardamom)

Melt honey, sugar, and butter together. Stir all other ingredients together with the honey mixture. Roll out to $1/2$-inch thickness. Cut into rectangles.

Macaroon Batter

3 egg whites
1 tbs lemon juice
$2/3$ cup sugar
$1/2$ tsp vanilla extract
9 oz ground almonds

Beat egg whites and lemon juice until very stiff. Drizzle in sugar and vanilla and continue beating until glossy. Fold in almonds.

Secrets to success: Use a clean, grease-free bowl. Fold in almonds gradually. Use 2 tsp to transfer small mounds of batter onto a parchment-lined baking sheet.

Troubleshooting — What to do if...

... The frosting is lumpy

➤ Put the frosting through a tea strainer, preferably one spoonful or one drop at a time.

... The frosting is too thick

➤ Carefully stir in a little liquid.

... The frosting is too runny

➤ Stir in a little sifted powdered sugar, one teaspoonful at a time.

... The couverture* is too runny

➤ Add and melt in 1–2 tsp coconut fat. This will make the couverture glossier and easier to spread.

*Coating chocolate is very glossy. It contains about 32% cocoa butter and forms a thin coating. Available at specialty stores.

... The cookie dough is too dry and crumbly

➤ Beat 1 egg yolk or 1 tbs butter into dough and set it aside for 15 minutes.

... The cookie dough is too soft and sticky

➤ Refrigerate the dough for another hour. Immediately after kneading, shape into smaller portions and then remove each portion from the refrigerator, one at a time, right when you're ready to process it.
➤ Carefully knead in a little more flour.

... The cookie batter is too soft

➤ Refrigerate the batter for 1 hour. This will harden the butter component so the batter will be easier to process.

... The cookies are hard and dry

➤ Sandwich pairs of cookies together with your favorite jam in between to make them wonderfully soft and moist.

... The macaroon batter is too runny

➤ Beat 1 egg white until stiff and fold into the mixture. Don't let the macaroon batter stand any longer— process it immediately!

5

Tools

For batter and dough: You'll need a kitchen scale to weigh the ingredients. It's best to have a large bowl for dough because you can mix it better and more cleanly in the bowl than on a pastry board. A hand mixer is a must.

For rolling out: Best is a large wooden or plastic pastry board. Specialty stores also carry thick plastic pastry mats and baking mats that you can simply roll up after baking. You'll need a wooden or marble rolling pin to roll out the dough.

For cut-out cookies: Cookie cutters are available in all shapes and sizes. Fluted pastry wheels are especially good for cutting dough into diamonds or squares.

For baking: Every kitchen needs 1 or 2 baking sheets. It makes no difference whether they're enameled, Teflon-coated, tinplate, or black-plated.

For the baking sheet: Line the baking sheet with parchment paper or special baking foil. The cookies won't stick and you can reuse the paper. The major advantage is that you won't be constantly washing baking sheets!

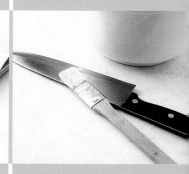

For brushing: Buy a good pastry brush for brushing egg or glaze onto cookies. To fill cookies with jam, all you need is a knife with a wide blade. Place your decorated and glazed cookies on parchment paper and let harden.

Decorating Made Easy

Melting chocolate or couverture

It's best to melt chocolate or couverture in a double boiler. To make your own, fill a medium-sized saucepan with ¾–1 inch of water and place it on the burner. Insert a heat-resistant bowl (for example, made of stainless steel) with a diameter slightly larger than that of a pan and place the chopped chocolate in a bowl. Slowly melt the chocolate over low heat, stirring frequently. Add a little coconut oil to semisweet chocolate couverture so it will be smooth and harden with a glossy finish (use 1–2 tbs coconut oil for ¾ cup couverture). If you have any chocolate or couverture left over, you can let it harden and store it in a screw-top jar.

Piping on designs

Place melted couverture in a small freezer bag and tie it closed. Cut a small piece off of one corner. Squeeze the couverture through the hole and onto the cookies.

Dipping

Dip baked goods all or partway into melted chocolate or couverture, wiping excess onto edge of bowl. Place them on aluminum foil or parchment paper to harden. Sprinkle with nuts, etc.

Frosting

Sift powdered sugar into a small bowl. Add flavored liquid of your preference (e.g., rum, lemon juice) and, flavoring if desired, and stir to form a smooth frosting. Spread onto cookies.

Star cookies

Spread cookies with white frosting. Place a small dollop of red jelly or jam (stirred until smooth) in the center. Use a toothpick to spread the jelly outward in a star shape.

The ABC's of Ingredients

Anise
Aniseed comes from the anise plant and is available whole or ground. Anise is a traditional ingredient used in Christmas baking throughout many countries. It has a sweet-spicy flavor that resembles licorice and is powerful and penetrating, so use it sparingly. Always buy anise fresh and use it up.

Candied fruits
These are fruits boiled in sugar (including candied lemon and orange peel, as well as candied cherries, dates, and ginger). Candied lemon peel is made from citrons and candied orange peel from the rind of bitter or Seville oranges. The peels are boiled in sugar syrup and then dried. Both are available in supermarkets,

> *Star anise is also a favorite Christmas decoration.*

as are candied cherries and ginger. You'll also find a mixture of chopped candied fruit for baking.

Cardamom
The pods on the cardamom stalks contain seeds that are ground and typically used as a Christmas spice. Cardamom has a strong and tangy flavor. Like all spices with essential oils, purchase only small amounts of the ground variety. Along with saffron and vanilla, cardamom is one of the most expensive spices in the world.

Cinnamon
Cinnamon, also sold as Ceylon cinnamon, is taken from the bark of the cinnamon tree. It is available in the form of cinnamon sticks or ground. Cinnamon has a spicy-sweet flavor with a pleasant bite. It is one of the traditional Christmas spices. Whole cinnamon sticks, which you can crush in a mortar or grind in a spice mill just before using, are better and more aromatic than ground cinnamon, which is produced from broken pieces.

Cloves
Cloves are the dried flower buds of the clove tree and are

> *Green cardamom has a much finer aroma than black.*

available whole or ground. They have a sweet, hot flavor and are extremely aromatic. Cloves are a typical ingredient in Christmas cookies. In a well-sealed container, whole cloves keep for years. Purchase ground cloves in very small quantities and always buy them fresh.

Coriander
Coriander comes from the seeds of the coriander plant, which are available whole, cracked, or ground. It is extremely aromatic with a sweet-spicy flavor. Coriander is used as a spice in certain types of bread, baked goods, fish, liqueurs, and in Asian cuisine.

Couverture
Couverture is made from pure cocoa and sugar and contains more cocoa butter than chocolate, which makes it runnier when melted and

8

more stable when solidified. Couverture is available in various flavors, including semisweet chocolate, milk chocolate, and white and is used to coat and decorate cookies. For more ideas and tips on decorating with couverture, see page 7.

Ginger

Ginger is a rhizome from a Southeast Asian plant. It is available fresh as a root, ground into powder, or candied, which may also be chocolate-covered. Ginger has a sweet, hot flavor. For cookies, we generally use the ground or candied form.

Marzipan

Marzipan is made from shelled, peeled almonds and powdered sugar, plus a few bitter almonds to give it its characteristic aroma. Marzipan is available in supermarkets in tightly sealed blocks. The best way to process marzipan is to roll it out between two sheets of plastic wrap.

Nutmeg

The kernel of this peach-like stone fruit produced by the tropical nutmeg tree is available whole or grated.

The same fruit provides both mace (the thin orange-to-crimson-colored, lace-like network covering the seed) and nutmeg (the seed itself). The outer peel is not used. Freshly grated nutmeg has a very intense and spicy flavor and is used in baked goods, sauces and potato, and vegetable dishes. For fine baked goods, ground mace is preferred because of its more delicate aroma. Ground mace is available in stores.

When using nutmeg, you're much better off using the whole nuts than the ground spice. Note that large and undamaged nuts have the best aroma. If stored in a dry container, whole nutmeg keeps for years.

Pistachios

These green, oily seeds of the pistachio tree are available whole and, in well-stocked supermarkets, chopped. Their flavor is similar to almonds, and both chopped and whole pistachios are favorites for decorating baked goods. Finely ground pistachios can also be used as a baking ingredient.

Poppy seeds

These tiny, oily seeds taken from poppy pods are mainly used for baked goods and confectionery. Whole poppy seeds are also sprinkled on bread and rolls but otherwise, the seeds are usually ground. You can grind poppy seeds yourself using a blender, a powerful hand blender, or a

> *The red covering surrounding nutmeg is dried to produce mace.*

grain mill; or have them ground at your health food store. Ground poppy seeds quickly become rancid and won't keep, but you can freeze them.

Vanilla

These boiled and dried pods from an orchid plant are available whole (usually called beans), ground, and as vanilla extract. You can also make your own vanilla sugar: Store 1 vanilla bean in a jar of sugar for several weeks, shaking it daily.

Cookie Dough— Endlessly Versatile

When you bake cookies from dough, almost anything is possible! Whether you roll it out for traditional cut-out cookies, roll it into balls, shape it into crescents, or cut it into bars right on the baking sheet, the result is always sinfully delicious!

11	Almond Cookies
11	Nut Balls
13	Raspberry Stars
13	Strawberry Circles
13	Nougat Rounds
15	Hazelnut Bites
15	Walnut Rounds
15	Heidesand Cookies
17	Linzer Cookies
17	Lemon Triangles
17	Ginger Hearts
19	Cashew Sticks
19	Vanilla Crescents
21	Three-Tiered Chocolate Cookies
21	Streusel Hearts
21	Orange Moons
23	Hazelnut Corners
23	Coconut Bars
24	Coffee Flowers
24	Marzipan Slices
26	Almond Sticks
26	Pistachio Pinwheels
28	Star Sandwich Cookies
28	Christmas Bites

Quick Recipes

Almond Cookies

MAKES 100 COOKIES

➤ 2 cups flour | ²/₃ cup sugar
 ¹/₂ cup softened butter | 2 eggs
 1¹/₂ cups skinned, halved almonds

1 | Knead the flour, sugar, butter and 1 egg into smooth dough, wrap in plastic wrap, and refrigerate. Line a baking sheet with parchment paper.

2 | Preheat the oven to 400°F. Whisk 1 egg. Roll out dough to the thickness of the back of a knife blade. Cut out cookies and transfer to a baking sheet. Brush with egg, place half an almond on top of each, and bake in the oven (middle rack) for 7–8 minutes until lightly browned.

Nut Balls

MAKES 50 COOKIES

➤ ¹/₂ cup softened butter | ³/₄ cup nougat paste | 1 egg | 2¹/₂ cups flour 1 dash cinnamon | ¹/₂ tsp baking powder | 1 tsp vanilla extract | 50 macadamia nuts | ¹/₂ cup sugar

1 | Preheat the oven to 375°F. Knead the butter, nougat, egg, flour, cinnamon, baking powder, and vanilla into dough. Line a baking sheet with parchment paper.

2 | Divide the dough into batches. Shape into rolls and cut into 50 pieces. Shape each piece into a ball, press 1 nut into a center and smooth over. Place balls on the baking sheet and bake in the oven (middle rack) for 10–12 minutes. Roll hot balls in sugar and serve.

Fruity | Fast
Raspberry Stars

MAKES 100 COOKIES

- 2 cups flour
  1/2 cup sugar
  1/2 cup softened butter
  1 egg
  2 cups powdered sugar
  4 tbs lemon juice
  2 tbs raspberry jam

🕐 Prep time: 50 minutes
🕐 Baking time: 8–10 minutes
➤ Calories/cookie: About 35

1 | Knead the flour, sugar, butter, and egg into a dough, wrap in plastic wrap, and refrigerate.

2 | Preheat the oven to 400°F. Roll out the dough to a thickness of 1/4-inch, cut out stars, and transfer to a baking sheet. Bake in the oven (middle rack) for 8–10 minutes until lightly browned.

3 | Combine powdered sugar, lemon juice and 1 tbs jam to form a frosting and spread onto the cookies. Use the remaining 1 tbs jam to drop a dollop of jam onto the center of each star and stir it into the frosting with a toothpick.

Inexpensive
Strawberry Circles

MAKES 100 COOKIES

- 4 cups flour
  1 cup sugar
  1 cup softened butter
  3 eggs
  1 tsp vanilla extract
  1 1/4 cups strawberry jam
  Powdered sugar for dusting

🕐 Prep time: 1 hour and 20 minutes
🕐 Baking time: 10 minutes
➤ Calories/cookie: About 60

1 | Knead the flour, sugar, butter, eggs, and vanilla into smooth dough, wrap in plastic wrap, and refrigerate.

2 | Preheat the oven to 400°F. Roll out dough to the thickness of the back of a knife blade. Cut out an equal number of round cookies and rings of the same diameter. Transfer cookies to a baking sheet and bake in the oven (middle rack) for 10 minutes until lightly browned.

3 | Stir jam until smooth. Spread onto all the round cookies and place the rings on top. Dust with powdered sugar.

Crunchy | Easy
Nougat Rounds

MAKES 100 COOKIES

- 4 cups flour
  1 cup sugar
  1 cup softened butter
  2 eggs
  1 cup hazelnut-nougat spread (e.g., Nutella)
  1 cup hazelnut couverture

🕐 Prep time: 1 hour and 20 minutes
🕐 Baking time: 8–10 minutes
➤ Calories/cookie: About 70

1 | Knead the flour, sugar, butter, and eggs into a dough. Wrap and refrigerate.

2 | Preheat oven to 400°F. Roll out dough in several batches to 1/8-inch thickness. Cut out round cookies of equal diameter. Transfer cookies to a baking sheet and bake (middle rack) for 8–10 minutes until lightly browned. Let cool.

3 | Spread hazelnut-nougat on round. Place top on cookie and top with melted couverture.

Inexpensive | Aromatic

Hazelnut Bites

MAKES 80 COOKIES

➤ 1 egg
   1 2/3 cups flour
   2 cups ground hazelnuts
   1 cup powdered sugar
   3/4 cup softened butter
   1 cup chopped hazelnuts

🕐 Prep time: 50 minutes
🕐 Baking time: 8–10 minutes
➤ Calories/cookie: About 70

1 | Separate the egg and set aside. Knead the flour, ground hazelnuts, powdered sugar, butter and egg yolk, and form smooth dough. Shape into rolls 1 inch in diameter, wrap in plastic wrap, and refrigerate.

2 | Preheat the oven to 400°F. Whisk egg white. Spread chopped hazelnuts on a plate. Brush egg white onto dough and then roll in hazelnuts. Cut into slices 1/4-inch thick and transfer to a baking sheet. Bake in the oven (middle rack) for 8–10 minutes until lightly browned.

For Gourmets

Walnut Rounds

MAKES 80 COOKIES

➤ 2 cups flour
   1 1/3 cups coarsely ground walnuts
   1/4 cup sugar
   3/4 cup softened butter
   1 egg
   3 dashes cinnamon
   1 dash cloves
   2 cups powdered sugar
   2 tbs rum
   80 walnut halves

🕐 Prep time: 1 hour
🕐 Baking time: 12–15 minutes
➤ Calories/cookie: About 75

1 | Knead the flour, walnuts, sugar, butter, egg, 1 dash cinnamon, and cloves into dough. Shape into rolls 1 inch in diameter, wrap in plastic wrap, and refrigerate.

2 | Preheat the oven to 400°F. Cut rolls into slices 1-inch thick and transfer to a baking sheet. Bake in the oven (middle rack) for 12–15 minutes until golden.

3 | Combine powdered sugar, cinnamon, and rum to form a frosting. Spread onto cookies and top each with 1 walnut.

Traditional | Fast

Heidesand Cookies

MAKES 100 COOKIES

➤ 3/4 cup softened butter
   3/4 cup powdered sugar
   1/2 tsp vanilla extract
   1/4 cup marzipan
   Grated zest from 1/2 organic lemon
   1 cup flour
   1 egg
   1 cup sugar

🕐 Prep time: 40 minutes
🕐 Baking time: 8–10 minutes
➤ Calories/cookie: About 40

1 | Process butter, powdered sugar, vanilla, marzipan, and lemon zest into a smooth mixture. Shape into rolls 1 inch in diameter, wrap in plastic wrap, and refrigerate.

2 | Preheat the oven to 400°F. Whisk egg. Spread sugar on a plate. Brush egg onto dough and then roll in sugar. Cut into slices 1/4-inch thick, and place slices on a baking sheet with adequate spacing between them. Bake in the oven (middle rack) for 8–10 minutes until golden.

Traditional

Linzer Cookies

MAKES 90 COOKIES

➤ 2¹/₂ cups flour
  1 cup sugar
  1¹/₄ cups ground hazelnuts
  1 tsp cocoa
  1 tsp cinnamon
  1 dash cloves
  1 cup softened butter
  2 eggs
  1 tbs milk
  1¹/₄ cups raspberry jam

🕐 Prep time: 1 hour
🕐 Baking time: 8–10 minutes
➤ Calories/cookie: About 60

1 | Knead the flour, sugar, hazelnuts, cocoa, cinnamon, cloves, butter, and 1 egg into dough and refrigerate.

2 | Preheat the oven to 400°F. Whisk together remaining 1 egg and milk. Roll out dough to ¹/₈-inch thickness. Cut out round cookies and rings of the same size. Transfer cookies to a baking sheet. Brush rings with the egg-milk mixture. Bake (middle rack) for 8–10 minutes.

3 | Stir jam until smooth, and spread onto round cookies and top with rings.

Fruity

Lemon Triangles

MAKES 100 COOKIES

➤ 2¹/₂ cups flour
  ¹/₂ cup sugar
  ³/₄ cup ground almonds
  Zest from 1 lemon
  ³/₄ cup softened butter
  1 egg
  1¹/₄ cups currant jelly
  2 cups powdered sugar
  3 tbs lemon juice

🕐 Prep time: 1 hour
🕐 Baking time: 8–10 minutes
➤ Calories/cookie: About 50

1 | Knead the flour, sugar, almonds, lemon zest, butter, and egg into a smooth dough, wrap in plastic wrap, and refrigerate.

2 | Preheat oven to 400°F. Roll out dough to ¹/₈-inch thickness. Cut into triangles and place on a baking sheet. Bake (middle rack) for 8–10 minutes and let cool.

3 | Stir jelly until smooth and spread onto one half and top with other cookie. Combine powdered sugar, lemon juice, and frost.

Spicy

Ginger Hearts

MAKES 100 COOKIES

➤ 4 cups flour
  1¹/₄ cups sugar
  ¹/₂ tsp vanilla extract
  1¹/₄ cups ground hazelnuts
  1 tsp ginger
  3 eggs
  1 cup softened butter
  ¹/₂ cup candied ginger, finely chopped

🕐 Prep time: 1 hour
🕐 Baking time: 8–10 minutes
➤ Calories/cookie: About 60

1 | Knead the flour, sugar, vanilla, hazelnuts, ginger, 2 eggs, and butter to form dough, wrap in plastic wrap, and refrigerate.

2 | Preheat oven to 400°F. Whisk remaining 1 egg. Roll out dough to ¹/₈-inch thickness. Cut out hearts and transfer to a baking sheet. Brush with egg and sprinkle with diced ginger. Bake in the oven (middle rack) for 8–10 minutes until lightly browned.

Fast | Easy
Cashew Sticks

MAKES 75 COOKIES

➤ 2 cups flour
  $1/3$ cup sugar
  1 pinch salt
  $3/4$ cup chopped, unsalted cashews
  2 dashes coriander
  1 dash cinnamon
  $2/3$ cup softened butter
  1 egg
  4 oz milk chocolate or couverture

🕐 Prep time: 50 minutes
🕐 Baking time: 10–12 minutes
➤ Calories/cookie: About 50

1 | Knead the flour, sugar, salt, cashews, coriander, cinnamon, butter, and egg into a smooth dough, wrap in plastic wrap, and refrigerate.

2 | Preheat the oven to 400°F. Shape dough into rolls $1/2$ inch in diameter. Cut into pieces $2 1/2$-inches long and transfer to a baking sheet. Bake in the oven (middle rack) for 10–12 minutes and let cool.

3 | Melt chocolate. Dip one end of the cookies halfway into the chocolate. Place on waxed paper and let harden.

Traditional | Easy
Vanilla Crescents

MAKES 70 COOKIES

➤ 2 cups flour
  1 dash baking powder
  $2/3$ cup sugar
  1 tsp vanilla extract
  2 eggs
  $3/4$ cup softened butter
  $1 1/4$ cups ground hazelnuts
➤ For the topping:
  $1/4$ cup sugar
  2 tsp vanilla extract

🕐 Prep time: 50 minutes
🕐 Baking time: 12–15 minutes
➤ Calories/cookie: About 60

1 | Knead the flour, baking powder, sugar, vanilla, eggs, butter, and hazelnuts into dough. Wrap dough in plastic wrap and refrigerate.

2 | Preheat the oven to 400°F. Shape dough into rolls $3/4$ inch in diameter. Cut into pieces $1/2$-inch long and roll the pieces into little cylinders with tapered ends. Bend into crescents and transfer to a baking sheet. Bake in the oven (middle rack) for 12–15 minutes until lightly browned.

3 | In a bowl, combine sugar and vanilla, and dip the tops of the hot crescents into this mixture.

➤ Variation:
➤ **Chocolate Crescents**

Mix 1 cup flour, $1/2$ cup powdered sugar, 2 tbs cocoa, $1/2$ tsp cinnamon, $1/4$ cup grated chocolate, $1/2$ cup softened butter, and 2 eggs into dough. Shape and bake just like the Vanilla Crescents recipe. For decoration, melt 8 oz white chocolate or couverture. Dip the tips of the crescents first into the white chocolate and then into chopped pistachios.

Traditional with a Twist

Three-Tiered Chocolate Cookies

MAKES 100 COOKIES

➤ 3¹/₂ cups flour
2 tbs cocoa
1 tsp baking powder
²/₃ cup sugar
2 eggs
1 cup softened butter
¹/₂ cup ground hazelnuts
1 cup raspberry jam
Powdered sugar for dusting

🕐 Prep time: Over 1 hour
🕐 Baking time: 8–10 minutes
➤ Calories/cookie: About 50

1 | Knead the flour, cocoa, baking powder, sugar, eggs, butter, and hazelnuts into smooth dough. Cover dough and refrigerate.

2 | Preheat the oven to 400°F. Roll out dough to ¹/₈-inch and cut out rounds of three sizes. Transfer cookies to a baking sheet and bake for 8–10 minutes.

3 | Stack cookies of three sizes, spreading raspberry jam to hold them together. Dust with powdered sugar.

Aromatic

Streusel Hearts

MAKES 80 COOKIES

➤ 2 cups flour
1 tbs cocoa
1 tsp baking powder
¹/₄ cup sugar
1 egg
¹/₂ cup softened butter
1 cup currant jelly
➤ For the streusel:
¹/₃ cup melted butter
1 cup flour
¹/₄ cup sugar
¹/₂ tsp vanilla extract

🕐 Prep time: Over 1 hour
🕐 Baking time: 8–10 minutes
➤ Calories/cookie: About 50

1 | Knead the flour, cocoa, baking powder, sugar, egg, and butter into a smooth dough. Wrap the dough in plastic wrap and refrigerate.

2 | Preheat oven to 400°F. Combine all streusel ingredients. Roll out the dough to 1-inch thickness, cut out hearts, and transfer to a baking sheet. Stir jelly until smooth, spread onto cookies, and sprinkle with streusel. Bake for 8–10 minutes.

Easy

Orange Moons

MAKES 75 COOKIES

➤ 2 cups flour
1 tbs cocoa
1 tsp baking powder
¹/₄ cup sugar
Grated zest from ¹/₂ orange
1 egg
¹/₂ cup softened butter
3 tbs ground almonds
1³/₄ cups powdered sugar
3 tbs orange juice

🕐 Prep time: 1 hour
🕐 Baking time: 8–10 minutes
➤ Calories/cookie: About 40

1 | Knead the flour, cocoa, baking powder, sugar, orange zest, egg, butter, and almonds into dough. Wrap in plastic and refrigerate.

2 | Preheat the oven to 400°F. Roll out the dough in batches to ¹/₈-inch, cut out crescents, and transfer to a baking sheet. Bake (middle rack) for 8–10 minutes and let cool.

3 | Combine powdered sugar and orange juice to frost moons.

Easy

Hazelnut Corners

MAKES 80 COOKIES

- 2 cups flour
  1/4 cup sugar
  3/4 cup softened butter
  1 egg
- For the topping:
  2/3 cup softened butter
  1 1/2 cups powdered sugar
  2 eggs
  1 3/4 cups ground hazelnuts
  1 tsp cinnamon
  8 oz semisweet chocolate or couverture
  Butter or cooking spray for the baking sheet

- Prep time: 45 minutes
- Baking time: 20–25 minutes
- Calories/cookie: About 90

1 | Preheat the oven to 400°F. Grease the baking sheet with butter or cooking spray. Knead the flour, sugar, butter and egg into smooth dough, and roll out onto the baking sheet. Pierce dough numerous times with a fork.

3 | For the topping, combine butter, powdered sugar, eggs, hazelnuts and cinnamon, and spread onto the dough. Bake in the oven (middle rack) for 20–25 minutes until lightly browned. Cut into triangles while still warm and remove from the baking sheet to cool.

3 | Melt the chocolate in a double boiler. Dip two corners of each cookie into the chocolate, place on waxed paper, and let harden.

Aromatic | Inexpensive

Coconut Bars

MAKES 80 COOKIES

- 2 cups flour
  1/4 cup sugar
  3/4 cup butter
  1 egg
- For the topping:
  2/3 cup butter
  1 1/2 cups powdered sugar
  4 1/2 cups grated coconut
  Grated zest from 1 orange
- For decoration:
  8 oz semisweet chocolate or couverture
  Butter or cooking spray for the baking sheet

- Prep time: 50 minutes
- Baking time: 20–25 minutes
- Calories/cookie: About 90

1 | Preheat the oven to 400°F. Grease the baking sheet with butter or cooking spray. Knead flour, sugar, butter and egg into dough, and roll out onto the baking sheet. Pierce dough numerous times with a fork.

2 | Melt the butter in a large saucepan. Stir in powdered sugar, grated coconut, and orange zest. Spread mixture onto the dough. Bake in the oven (middle rack) for 20–25 minutes until lightly browned and let cool.

3 | Melt the chocolate in a double boiler. With a spoon, drizzle chocolate over the top of the cake in an irregular pattern. Let the chocolate harden and cut into 1-inch wide by 2-inch long bars.

Delicately Bitter

Coffee Flowers

MAKES 90 COOKIES

➤ 2¾ cups flour
¾ cup softened butter
⅔ cup sugar
1 tsp vanilla extract
2 eggs
¼ tsp baking powder
2 tsp instant cappuccino mix (any brand)
⅓ cup grated chocolate
1½ tbs instant coffee
2⅔ cups powdered sugar
90 chocolate-covered espresso beans

⏱ Prep time: 1 hour
⏱ Baking time: 8–10 minutes
➤ Calories/cookie: About 70

1 | Knead the flour, butter, sugar, vanilla, eggs, baking powder, cappuccino mix, and grated chocolate into smooth dough. Wrap the dough in plastic wrap and refrigerate.

2 | Preheat the oven to 400°F. Roll out dough in several batches to 1-inch thickness. Cut out flowers and transfer to a baking sheet. Bake in the oven (middle rack) for 8–10 minutes and let cool.

3 | Dissolve instant coffee in 6 tbs hot water. Combine coffee and powdered sugar to form a thick frosting. Spread onto cooled cookies and top each one with a chocolate-covered espresso bean.

For Gourmets

Marzipan Slices

MAKES 60 COOKIES

➤ 2¾ cups flour
1¼ cups powdered sugar
1 cup ground hazelnuts
½ cup grated chocolate
¾ cup softened butter
2 eggs
➤ For the filling:
2 eggs
1¼ cups marzipan
➤ For the frosting:
1¾ cups powdered sugar
1 tsp cinnamon
3 tbs rum (may substitute water)

⏱ Prep time: 50 minutes
⏱ Baking time: 20–25 minutes
➤ Calories/cookie: About 120

1 | Knead the flour, powdered sugar, hazelnuts, grated chocolate, butter, and eggs into a smooth dough. Wrap the dough in plastic wrap and refrigerate.

2 | Preheat the oven to 350°F. Separate eggs. Knead marzipan and egg whites into a smooth mixture. Whisk egg yolks separately. In another bowl, combine powdered sugar, cinnamon, and rum to form a frosting.

3 | Roll out dough in several batches on a lightly floured work surface to ⅛-inch thickness. With the aid of a ruler, cut into strips 2-inches wide. Transfer 1 strip to the baking sheet. Using 2 tsp, distribute a narrow strip of marzipan down the middle. Brush edges with egg yolk, place the second strip of dough on top, and press the edges together firmly. Repeat this procedure with the remaining strips of dough. Bake in the oven (middle rack) for 20–25 minutes.

4 | Spread the frosting onto the marzipan cake while still hot. Remove from the baking sheet and cut crosswise into slices ½-inch thick.

Photo top: **Coffee Flowers**   *Photo bottom:* **Marzipan Slices** ➤

Impressive
Almond Sticks

MAKES 95 COOKIES

- **2 eggs**
  3¹/₄ cups flour
  4 tsp baking powder
  1 cup sugar
  1 tsp vanilla extract
  ³/₄ cup softened butter
  1 tbs milk
  1 cup sliced almonds
- **For decoration:**
  8 oz semisweet chocolate or couverture
  1 cup red currant jelly

🕐 Prep time: 1 hour and 10 minutes
🕐 Baking time: 8–10 minutes
➤ Calories/cookie: About 65

1 | Separate 1 egg and set aside egg white. Knead the flour, baking powder, sugar, vanilla, the remaining whole egg, the egg yolk, and butter into a dough. Wrap in plastic wrap and refrigerate.

2 | Preheat the oven to 350°F. Whisk together egg white and milk. Roll out dough in several batches to ¹/₈-inch thickness. Cut into 1-inch wide by 2-inch long strips and transfer to a baking sheet. Brush with egg-milk mixture and sprinkle with sliced almonds. Bake in the oven (middle rack) for 8–10 minutes until lightly browned and let cool.

3 | Melt the chocolate in a double boiler. Stir currant jelly until smooth. Spread onto half the cookies and top with remaining cookies. Dip both ends of cookies into the chocolate, place on parchment paper, and let harden.

For Gourmets
Pistachio Pinwheels

MAKES 60 COOKIES

- **2 cups flour**
  ²/₃ cup sugar
  ¹/₂ tsp vanilla extract
  1 egg
  ¹/₂ cup softened butter
- **For the filling:**
  1¹/₄ cups marzipan
  2 egg whites
  ¹/₂ cup ground pistachios

🕐 Prep time: 50 minutes
🕐 Baking time: 8–10 minutes
➤ Calories/cookie: About 70

1 | Knead the flour, sugar, vanilla, egg and butter into a smooth dough, wrap in plastic wrap, and refrigerate.

2 | Knead the marzipan, egg whites, and pistachios into a smooth mixture. Roll out dough to ¹/₈-inch thickness and cut into 10-inch wide by 14-inch long rectangles. Spread with pistachio-marzipan mixture and starting from a long side of the rectangle, roll up dough. Wrap and refrigerate for 2–3 hours.

3 | Preheat the oven to 400°F. Using a sharp knife, cut rolls into slices ¹/₄-inch thick, and place slices on a baking sheet with adequate spacing between them. Bake in the oven (middle rack) for 8–10 minutes until lightly browned.

Photo top: **Almond Sticks**   *Photo bottom:* **Pistachio Pinwheels** ➤

Aromatic
Star Sandwich Cookies

MAKES 50 COOKIES

➤ 1/2 cup pecans

2 cups flour

2/3 cup brown sugar

1/2 tsp vanilla extract

1 egg

1/2 cup softened butter

➤ For the filling and decoration:

8 oz milk chocolate or couverture

3/4 cup plum butter

1 tbs rum (optional)

🕐 Prep time: 1 hour and 10 minutes

🕐 Baking time: 8–10 minutes

➤ Calories/cookie: About 90

1 | Grind the pecans finely. Knead the flour, sugar, vanilla, pecans, egg and butter into a smooth dough, wrap in plastic wrap, and refrigerate.

2 | Preheat the oven to 400°F. Line a baking sheet with parchment paper. Roll out dough in batches to 1/8-inch thickness. Cut out stars and transfer to the baking sheet. Bake in the oven (middle rack) for 8–10 minutes and let cool.

3 | Melt the chocolate in a double boiler. Combine plum butter with rum if desired and stir until smooth. Spread this mixture onto half the cookies and top with remaining cookies. Dip the points of the stars into the chocolate, place on parchment paper, and let harden.

Impressive
Christmas Bites

MAKES 100 COOKIES

➤ 3 3/4 cups flour

1 tsp baking powder

2/3 cup sugar

2 tbs cocoa

1/2 cup ground almonds

1 tsp cinnamon

1/4 tsp cloves

2 eggs

1 cup softened butter

➤ For the filling and decoration:

8 oz semisweet chocolate or couverture

1 cup apricot jam

🕐 Prep time: 1 hour and 5 minutes

🕐 Baking time: 8–10 minutes

➤ Calories/cookie: About 60

1 | Knead the flour, baking powder, sugar, cocoa, almonds, cinnamon, cloves, eggs and butter into a smooth dough, wrap in plastic wrap, and refrigerate.

2 | Preheat the oven to 400°F. Roll out dough in batches to 1/8-inch thickness. Cut out round cookies and transfer to a baking sheet. Bake in the oven (middle rack) for 8–10 minutes and let cool.

3 | Melt the chocolate in a double boiler. Stir apricot jam until smooth. Spread jam onto half the cookies and top with remaining cookies. Dip the cookies halfway into the chocolate, place on waxed paper, and let harden.

TIP Christmas Bites are also delicious with orange marmalade.

Cookie Batter—
Sometimes Twirled,
Sometimes Spread Flat

With these cookies, a spoon does most of the stirring and kneading for you. Whether you spread it out on a baking sheet, put it through a grinder, or pipe it out of a pastry bag, the result is always irresistible!

31   Poppy-Seed Amaretto Kisses

31   Chocolate Squares

33   Chocolate Sticks

33   Orange Marzipan Wreaths

33   Eggnog S's

35   Orange Tongues

35   Pecan Mounds

36   Peanut Bars

36   Fruit Squares

38   Mocha Triangles

38   Ginger Bars

41   Tree Cake Cubes

Quick Recipes

Poppy Seed Amaretto Kisses

MAKES 80 COOKIES

➤ ¹/₄ cup poppy seeds | 20 sour cherries (from a jar) | ¹/₂ cup softened butter | ¹/₂ cup powdered sugar | 1 egg | 1 tbs Amaretto | 1¹/₄ cups flour | ¹/₂ tsp baking powder

1 | Preheat the oven to 400°F. Grind poppy seeds. Cut cherries into quarters, making sure stems and pits are removed. Cream butter and sugar together. Add egg and Amaretto. Stir in flour, baking powder, and poppy seeds.

2 | Place the batter in a pastry bag with a large plain tip. Pipe onto a baking sheet in walnut-sized mounds and top each with a quarter cherry. Bake in the oven (middle rack) for 8–10 minutes.

Chocolate Squares

MAKES 80 COOKIES

➤ 1 cup softened butter | ²/₃ cup sugar | 3 eggs | ³/₄ cup grated chocolate | 2 cups ground hazelnuts | 2 cups flour | ¹/₂ tsp baking powder | ¹/₂ tsp cinnamon | 1 tbs cocoa | 2 cups powdered sugar | 3 tbs lemon juice | Butter or cooking spray for the baking sheet

1 | Preheat oven to 400°F. Grease a baking sheet. Cream together butter, sugar, and eggs. Stir in grated chocolate, hazelnuts, flour, baking powder, cinnamon, and cocoa. Spread batter on baking sheet to ³/₄-inch thickness and bake for 20–25 minutes.

2 | Combine powdered sugar and lemon juice for frosting. Spread onto the hot cake. Cool and cut into squares.

31

Easy

Chocolate Sticks

MAKES 80 COOKIES

➤ 1 cup softened butter
1 cup powdered sugar
2 eggs
1^2/$_3$ cups flour
2 tbs cocoa
^{1}/$_2$ tsp cinnamon
^{1}/$_2$ tsp baking powder
1 cup ground almonds
8 oz white chocolate or couverture
1 cup hazelnut-nougat cream (e.g., Nutella brand)

🕐 Prep time: 1 hour
🕐 Baking time: 8–10 minutes
➤ Calories/cookie: About 80

1 | Preheat oven to 400°F. Cream butter, powdered sugar, and eggs. Stir in flour, cocoa, cinnamon, baking powder, and almonds. Place batter in a pastry bag with a large star tip and pipe onto a baking sheet in 2-inch strips. Bake (middle rack) for 8–10 minutes and let cool.

2 | Melt white chocolate in a double boiler. Spread hazelnut nougat cream onto half the cookies and top with remaining cookies. Dip one end into the white chocolate.

Easy | Fast

Orange Marzipan Wreaths

MAKES 80 COOKIES

➤ ^{1}/$_2$ cup marzipan
^{1}/$_2$ cup softened butter
2 eggs
^{1}/$_4$ cup sugar
Zest from 1 orange
1^3/$_4$ cups flour
^{1}/$_3$ cup cornstarch
1 tsp baking powder
1^1/$_2$ cups powdered sugar
2 tbs orange juice

🕐 Prep time: 45 minutes
🕐 Baking time: 10–12 minutes
➤ Calories/cookie: About 40

1 | Preheat oven to 400°F. Stir marzipan, butter, eggs, and sugar until smooth. Add half the orange zest, flour, cornstarch, and baking powder. Place batter in a pastry bag with a star tip and pipe wreaths onto a baking sheet. Bake (middle rack) for 10–12 minutes and let cool.

2 | Combine powdered sugar and orange juice. Dip wreath tops into the glaze and sprinkle with remaining orange zest.

Best When Fresh

Eggnog S's

MAKES 100 COOKIES

➤ 1 cup softened butter
1 cup powdered sugar
^{1}/$_2$ tsp vanilla extract
2 eggs
^{1}/$_2$ cup eggnog
1 tbs brandy (optional)
1^2/$_3$ cups flour
1 tsp baking powder
2 cups ground hazelnuts
➤ For decoration:
2 cups powdered sugar
1 tbs lemon juice
^{1}/$_4$ cup eggnog
1 tsp brandy (optional)
8 oz semisweet chocolate or couverture

🕐 Prep time: 50 minutes
➤ Calories/cookie: About 70

1 | Preheat oven to 400°F. Combine butter, powdered sugar, vanilla, eggs, eggnog, and if desired brandy, and flour, baking powder, and hazelnuts to form a batter. Place in a pastry bag and pipe "S" shapes onto a baking sheet. Bake for 10 minutes.

2 | Combine sugar, lemon juice, eggnog, and if desired, brandy for glaze. Melt chocolate. Dip one end into glaze and other into chocolate.

Best When Fresh

Orange Tongues

MAKES 70 COOKIES

- 1 cup softened butter
  1¼ cups powdered sugar
  2 eggs
  Grated zest from 2 oranges
  2½ cups flour
  1 tsp baking powder
  1 cup ground almonds
- For decoration:
  5 oz semisweet chocolate or couverture
  ½ cup orange marmalade
  1 tbs orange liqueur (optional)

🕐 Prep time: 50 minutes
🕐 Baking time: 10–12 minutes
➤ Calories/cookie: About 80

1 | Preheat the oven to 400°F. Cream together the butter, powdered sugar, eggs, and orange zest. With a dough hook, stir in flour, baking powder, and almonds. Place batter in a pastry bag with a large plain tip and pipe onto a baking sheet in 2-inch strips. Bake in the oven (middle rack) for 10–12 minutes and let cool.

2 | Melt the chocolate in a double boiler. Heat marmalade slightly and, if desired, stir with orange liqueur until smooth. Spread a thin coating of marmalade onto one end of the cookies and then dip this end into the chocolate.

TIP Another beautiful decoration for Orange Tongues is to sprinkle fine strips of zest from oranges onto the fresh melted chocolate.

Aromatic

Pecan Mounds

MAKES 30 COOKIES

- 1¼ cups pecans
  ½ cup softened butter
  ⅔ cup powdered sugar
  ½ tsp vanilla extract
  1 egg
  ¾ cup flour
  1 dash baking powder
  ¼ tsp cardamom
  8 oz milk chocolate or couverture
  30 pecan halves

🕐 Prep time: 50 minutes
🕐 Baking time: 10–12 minutes
➤ Calories/cookie: About 130

1 | Preheat oven to 400°F. Grind pecans. Cream together the butter, powdered sugar, vanilla, and egg. With a dough hook, stir in flour, baking powder, cardamom, and ground pecans.

2 | Place the batter in a pastry bag with a large plain tip and pipe onto a baking sheet in walnut-sized mounds. Bake in the oven (middle rack) for 10–12 minutes until lightly browned and let cool.

3 | Melt the chocolate in a double boiler. Place one thick dollop of chocolate on each cookie and top with 1 pecan half.

Fast

Peanut Bars

MAKES 60 COOKIES

- ➤ 1¼ cup unsalted peanuts
  - ½ cup softened butter
  - ¼ cup sugar
  - 2 eggs
  - ½ tsp cinnamon
  - Grated zest from ½ lemon
  - 1¼ cups flour
  - 1½ tsp baking powder
- ➤ For the topping:
  - 1 egg
  - 1 tbs milk
  - 2 tbs sugar
  - ½ tsp cinnamon
  - Butter or cooking spray for the baking sheet

- ⏱ Prep time: 45 minutes
- ⏱ Baking time: 15–20 minutes
- ➤ Calories/cookie: About 60

1 | In an ungreased pan, toast peanuts lightly, let cool, and chop coarsely. Grease a baking sheet with butter or cooking spray. Preheat oven to 400°F. Cream together the butter, sugar, and eggs. Fold in cinnamon, lemon zest, ¾ cup peanuts, flour, and baking powder. Spread batter onto the baking sheet to ¾-inch thickness.

2 | Whisk together egg and milk, and brush onto the batter. Combine remaining ½ cup peanuts, sugar and cinnamon, and sprinkle on top. Bake in the oven (middle rack) for 15–20 minutes until lightly browned. Let cool and using a sharp knife, cut into 1-inch wide by 2-inch long bars.

Traditional with a Twist

Fruit Squares

MAKES 60 COOKIES

- ➤ 3 eggs
  - ⅔ cup sugar
  - ¾ cup slivered almonds
  - ¾ cup chopped hazelnuts
  - 1 cup diced candied orange peel
  - 1 cup diced dried figs
  - 1 cup currants
  - 1 cup finely chopped dates
  - 1 cup flour
  - ½ tsp baking powder
  - ½ tsp cinnamon
- ➤ For decoration:
  - 8 oz semisweet chocolate or couverture
  - Butter or cooking spray for the baking sheet

- ⏱ Prep time: 45 minutes

- ⏱ Baking time: 30–35 minutes
- ➤ Calories/cookie: About 90

1 | Preheat the oven to 325°F. Grease a baking sheet with butter or cooking spray. Beat eggs and sugar until foamy. One at a time, add slivered almonds, hazelnuts, candied orange peel, figs, currants, dates, flour, baking powder, and cinnamon. Spread batter onto the baking sheet to ¾-inch thickness and bake in the oven (middle rack) for 30–35 minutes. Let cool.

2 | Melt the chocolate in a double boiler and spread onto the cake. Let harden and cut into 1-inch wide by 1-inch long squares.

Best When Fresh
Mocha Triangles

MAKES 70 COOKIES

- ➤ 1¼ cups softened butter
- 1 cup sugar
- 3 eggs
- 1 heaping tsp cinnamon
- 1 tsp cloves
- 1¼ cups chopped almonds
- ⅔ cup grated chocolate
- 3 cups flour
- 1½ tsp baking powder
- 7 tbs strong coffee
- ➤ For the topping:
- 1¼ cups powdered sugar
- ¼ cup grated chocolate
- Butter or cooking spray for the baking sheet

- 🕐 Prep time: 45 minutes
- 🕐 Baking time: 20–25 minutes
- ➤ Calories/cookie: About 110

1 | Preheat the oven to 400°F. Grease a baking sheet with butter or cooking spray. Cream together the butter, sugar, and eggs. Add cinnamon, cloves, almonds, grated chocolate, flour, baking powder, and 3 tbs coffee.

2 | Spread batter onto the baking sheet to ¾-inch thickness. Bake in the oven (middle rack) for 20–25 minutes and let cool.

3 | Combine powdered sugar and 4 tbs coffee to form a frosting. Spread frosting onto cake, sprinkle with grated chocolate, and let harden. Using a sharp knife, cut into triangles.

Aromatic | Fast
Ginger Bars

MAKES 50 COOKIES

- ➤ ½ cup candied ginger
- 1 cup softened butter
- ⅔ cup sugar
- 3 eggs
- 2 cups ground hazelnuts
- ½ cup chopped almonds
- ¾ cup grated chocolate
- 2 cups flour
- ½ tsp baking powder
- ➤ For the frosting:
- 2 cups powdered sugar
- 1 dash ground ginger
- 3 tbs lemon juice
- Butter or cooking spray for the baking sheet

- 🕐 Prep time: 35 minutes
- 🕐 Baking time: 20–25 minutes
- ➤ Calories/cookie: About 150

1 | Preheat the oven to 400°F. Grease a baking sheet with butter or cooking spray. Chop ginger very finely. Cream together the butter, sugar, and eggs. Stir in hazelnuts, almonds, grated chocolate, ginger, flour, and baking powder.

2 | Spread the batter onto the baking sheet to ¾-inch thickness. Bake in the oven (middle rack) for 20–25 minutes and let cool.

3 | Combine powdered sugar, ground ginger, and lemon juice to form a frosting and spread onto the cake. Let harden and then cut into 1-inch wide by 2-inch long bars.

- ➤ Variation:
  While still on the baking sheet, spread melted semisweet chocolate or couverture onto the cooled ginger cake. Then sprinkle finely chopped candied ginger onto the chocolate or couverture. Let harden and cut into squares.

Photo left: **Ginger Bars**   *Photo right:* **Mocha Triangles** ➤

Traditional | Takes More Time

Tree Cake Cubes

MAKES 60 COOKIES
(1 LOAF PAN, ABOUT
12-INCHES LONG)

➤ 1/2 cup apricot jam
   1/2 cup softened butter
   1 1/4 cups powdered sugar
   1/2 tsp vanilla extract
   3 eggs
   2 tbs cream
   1 cup flour
➤ For decoration:
   4 oz white chocolate
   or couverture
   4 oz semisweet chocolate
   or couverture
   4 oz milk chocolate
   or couverture
   Butter or cooking spray
   for pan

🕐 Prep time: 1 hour and
   10 minutes
🕐 Baking time: 3–4 minutes
   per layer
➤ Calories/cookie: About 80

1 | Preheat the oven to 475°F.
Thoroughly grease a loaf
pan. Heat apricot jam and
stir until smooth, or purée
if desired. Cream together
the butter, powdered sugar,
vanilla, and eggs. Add cream
and stir in flour.

2 | Spread 2–3 tbs batter onto
the bottom of the pan and
bake in the oven (middle
rack) for 3–4 minutes until
lightly browned. Spread
another 2–3 tbs batter on top
and bake 3–4 minutes. Spread
a thin layer of jam on top and

then another 2–3 tbs batter,
and bake 3–4 minutes. Repeat
this procedure until all the
batter is gone, spreading one
more layer with jam. Cool
cake in the pan.

3 | In a double boiler, melt
the three different types of
chocolate separately.

4 | Remove cake from the
pan and cut into slices 1-inch
thick. Cut slices into uniform
cubes. Using a fork, dip 20
tree cake cubes into each type
of chocolate and let harden
on parchment paper. Place
remaining chocolate in small
freezer bags, cut off a tiny
corner, and pipe onto
different colored cubes.

1 Spread batter

*Spread 2–3 tbs batter
in the pan so it just
covers the bottom.*

2 Cut into cubes

*Using a sharp knife,
cut cake slices into
uniform cubes.*

3 Chocolate or
couverture coating

*Using a fork, dip tree
cake cubes into melted
chocolate or couverture.*

German Gingersnap (Lebkuchen) Dough— A Taste of Christmas!

We know Christmas is coming when our house is filled with the delicious scents of anise, cardamom, coriander, nutmeg, cloves, and cinnamon—and when we are likewise filled with the most exquisite anticipation!

43 Chocolate Triangles

43 Spiced Almond Stars

45 German Gingersnaps (Lebkuchen)

45 Spiced Citrus Cookies

46 Honey Cake Pinwheels

46 Swiss Spice Cookies

48 Domino Stones

48 Honey Rum Cubes

50 Honey Cake Squares

50 Gingerbread

Quick Recipes

Chocolate Triangles

MAKES 45 COOKIES

➤ ²/₃ cup honey | ¼ cup brown sugar |
2 tbs vegetable oil | 1 egg | 1 tsp
cocoa | 6 drops rum extract | 1 dash
cardamom | 1 tsp cinnamon | 2 cups
flour | 3 tsp baking powder | ³/₄ cup
chopped hazelnuts | 8 oz semisweet
chocolate or couverture

1 | Preheat the oven to 400°F. Heat the
honey, sugar, and oil. Stir in egg, cocoa,
rum, cardamom, and cinnamon. Mix flour,
baking powder, and hazelnuts with the
honey mixture. Shape into 2 rolls (1 inch
in diameter) transfer to a baking sheet and
press flat. Bake in the oven (middle rack)
for 15–20 minutes and let cool.

2 | Melt the chocolate. Cut rolls into
triangles and dip into chocolate.

Spiced Almond Stars

MAKES 70 COOKIES

➤ 3¹/₃ cups flour | 1 tsp baking powder |
1 cup sugar | ¹/₂ tsp vanilla extract |
1 egg | ¹/₂ tsp cinnamon | 1 dash
cloves | 1 dash cardamom | 1¹/₄ cups
cold butter | 1 egg yolk | 1 tbs milk |
²/₃ cup sliced almonds

1 | Knead the flour, baking powder, sugar,
vanilla, egg, spices, and finely chopped
butter into a dough. Wrap the dough in
plastic wrap and refrigerate.

2 | Whisk together the egg yolk and milk.
Preheat the oven to 400°F. Roll out dough
to ³/₄-inch thickness. Cut out stars and
transfer to a baking sheet. Brush with
egg-milk mixture and sprinkle with
almonds. Bake in the oven (middle rack)
for 10–12 minutes.

43

Traditional | Aromatic

German Gingersnaps (Lebkuchen)

MAKES 50 COOKIES

➤ 4 eggs

$1^1/_4$ cups brown sugar

2 cups flour

$^1/_2$ cup chopped almonds

2 cups ground hazelnuts

$^2/_3$ cup diced candied orange peel

$^2/_3$ cup diced candied lemon peel

1 tsp cinnamon

$^1/_4$ tsp baking powder

1 dash cloves

1 dash cardamom

1 dash nutmeg

➤ For decoration:

2 cups powdered sugar

3 tbs lemon juice

50 skinned almonds

🕙 Prep time: 50 minutes

🕙 Standing time: 12 hours

🕙 Baking time: 18–20 minutes

➤ Calories/cookie: About 110

1 | Cream together the eggs and sugar. Add flour, chopped almonds, hazelnuts, candied orange peel, candied lemon peel, cinnamon, baking powder and remaining spices, and mix well.

2 | Place 2 tsp-sized mounds of dough on a baking sheet lined with parchment paper. Moisten your fingers, press mounds into shape. Let dry for 12 hours.

3 | Preheat the oven to 325°F. Bake in the oven (middle rack) for 18–20 minutes and let cool.

4 | Combine powdered sugar and lemon juice to form a frosting and spread onto the cookie. Place an almond on top of each cookie and let dry thoroughly.

Traditional | Easy

Spiced Citrus Cookies

MAKES 65 COOKIES

➤ $^2/_3$ cup brown rock sugar

$1^1/_2$ tsp baking powder

1 tbs rum (may substitute water)

$1^2/_3$ cups sugar beet syrup

$^1/_2$ cup brown sugar

5 cups flour

$^1/_2$ cup chopped candied orange peel

1 tsp each of cinnamon, anise, and coriander

1 dash cloves

3 tbs milk

🕙 Prep time: 50 minutes

🕙 Refrigeration time: 4 hours

🕙 Baking time: 10–12 minutes

➤ Calories/cookie: About 70

1 | Place rock sugar in a freezer bag and crush with a heavy flat-sided utensil. Dissolve baking powder in rum. Heat the sugar beet syrup, sugar, and 4 tbs water until the sugar dissolves.

2 | Combine flour, rock sugar, candied orange peel, cinnamon, anise, coriander, and cloves. Knead this mixture with baking powder and syrup into a dough. Wrap in plastic wrap and refrigerate for 4 hours.

3 | Preheat the oven to 350°F. Roll out dough to $^1/_8$-inch thickness. Cut into 1-inch by 3-inch rectangles and place 1 inch apart on a baking sheet. Brush with milk and bake in the oven (middle rack) for 10–12 minutes.

Impressive

Honey Cake Pinwheels

MAKES 40 COOKIES

- ½ cup honey

  ⅓ cup brown sugar

  ½ cup butter

  ⅓ cup semisweet chocolate or couverture

  1⅔ cups flour

  1 tsp baking powder

  2 tsp Lebkuchen spice (see p. 6 for recipe)
- For the filling:

  1¼ cups raisins

  3 tbs rum (optional)

  ¾ cup marzipan

  2 eggs

  ½ cup candied orange peel

- ⏱ Prep time: 45 minutes
- ⏱ Standing time: 1–2 hours
- ⏱ Baking time: 20–25 minutes
- Calories/cookie: About 120

1 | Heat the honey, sugar, and butter. Chop chocolate finely, add, and melt.

2 | Combine the flour, baking powder, Lebkuchen spice, and almonds. Knead together with honey mixture into a dough. Cover, and let stand at room temperature for 1–2 hours.

3 | In the meantime, soak raisins in rum if desired. Finely chop marzipan and whisk with eggs.

4 | Roll out dough into a 12–15-inch rectangle and spread with marzipan mixture. Drain raisins and sprinkle raisins and candied orange peel on the marzipan. Starting from a long side of the rectangle, roll up the dough, cover, and refrigerate for 1 hour.

5 | Preheat the oven to 350°F. Line a baking sheet with parchment paper. Cut roll into slices ¼-inch thick and place on the baking sheet. Bake in the oven (middle rack) for 20–25 minutes.

Traditional | Easy

Swiss Spice Cookies

MAKES 60 COOKIES

- 1 cup honey

  ½ cup brown sugar

  3¼ cups flour

  2 tsp baking powder

  1 tsp cinnamon

  ½ tsp cloves

  1 dash mace

  1 cup chopped hazelnuts

  ¼ cup diced candied orange peel

  ¼ cup diced candied lemon peel
- For the glaze:

  4 heaping tbs sugar

  Butter and flour for the baking sheet

- ⏱ Prep time: 40 minutes
- ⏱ Baking time: 15–20 minutes
- Calories/cookie: About 70

1 | Preheat the oven to 400°F. Butter a baking sheet and flour lightly.

2 | Heat the honey and brown sugar. In a large bowl, combine flour, baking powder, cinnamon, cloves, nutmeg, chopped hazelnuts, candied orange peel, and candied lemon peel. Add honey mixture and knead thoroughly. Roll out dough on the baking sheet to ½-inch thickness and bake in the oven (middle rack) for 15–20 minutes.

3 | For the glaze, boil sugar in 4 tbs water and spread onto the hot cake. Cut immediately into 1½-inch by 1½-inch squares and remove from baking sheet.

Traditional | Aromatic
Domino Stones

MAKES 45 COOKIES

- ➤ 2/3 cup honey
  1/2 cup brown sugar
  1/4 cup butter
  4 cups flour
  1/2 tsp baking powder
  1/2 tsp cinnamon
  1 dash cloves
  1 egg
- ➤ For the filling:
  3/4 cup currant jelly
  3/4 cup marzipan
  1 tbs rum (optional)
- ➤ For the coating:
  1 1/4 cups semisweet chocolate or couverture
  Butter or cooking spray for the baking sheet

🕐 Prep time: 1 hour
🕐 Baking time: 15 minutes
➤ Calories/cookie: About 140

1 | Preheat the oven to 400°F. Grease a baking sheet. Melt honey, sugar, and butter. Mix the flour, baking powder, cinnamon, and cloves with honey mixture and egg. Roll out dough on the baking sheet to 1/4-inch thickness, and bake (middle rack) for 15 minutes. Cut in half while hot.

2 | Heat jelly and stir until smooth. Spread a thin layer onto one half of the sheet. Mix the marzipan and rum, place between pieces of plastic wrap and roll out to the size of one half of the pan. Place on top of layer of jelly and spread with another layer of jelly. Place the second sheet on top and press together. Cut stack into cubes.

3 | Melt the chocolate and use to coat the cubes.

Easy | Fruity
Honey Rum Cubes

MAKES 60 COOKIES

- ➤ 3/4 cup apricot jam
  1 cup honey
  2/3 cup brown sugar
  1 egg
  1/2 tsp cinnamon
  1 dash cloves
  Grated zest from 1/2 orange
  1/2 cup chopped candied orange peel
  1/2 cup chopped almonds
  1/3 cup, plus 1 tbs milk
  3 cups flour
  2 tsp baking powder

- ➤ For the punch glaze:
  2 cups powdered sugar
  1 tbs lemon juice
  1 tbs rum
  Butter or cooking spray for the baking sheet

🕐 Prep time: 50 minutes
🕐 Baking time: 30–35 minutes
➤ Calories/cookie: About 80

1 | Preheat the oven to 350°F. Grease a baking sheet. Heat apricot jam, and stir or purée until smooth.

2 | Cream honey, sugar, and egg. Stir in cinnamon, cloves, orange zest, candied orange peel, almonds, and milk. Gently blend in flour and baking powder.

3 | Spread dough on baking sheet to 1/2-inch thickness, and bake (middle rack) for 30–35 minutes. While still hot, cut into uniform cubes, spread a thin layer of jam onto tops, and cut edges; let dry slightly.

4 | Sift powdered sugar and combine with lemon juice, rum, and 1 tbs warm water. Immediately spread on cubes.

Photo top: Domino Stones   Photo bottom: Honey Rum Cubes ➤

Fruity | Aromatic

Honey Cake Squares

MAKES 60 COOKIES

➤ 2$\frac{1}{4}$ cups honey
  $\frac{3}{4}$ cup butter
  1$\frac{1}{4}$ cups brown sugar
  5$\frac{1}{4}$ cups flour
  1 tsp baking powder
  4 tbs cocoa
  1 tsp cinnamon
  1 tsp cloves
  $\frac{1}{2}$ tsp cardamom
  Grated zest from 1 orange
  1 cup ground almonds
➤ For the filling:
  1$\frac{1}{2}$ cups apricot jam
  $\frac{3}{4}$ cup chopped candied orange peel
  1$\frac{1}{2}$ cups chopped almonds
  $\frac{3}{4}$ cup currants
➤ For the frosting:
  2$\frac{1}{4}$ cups powdered sugar
  $\frac{1}{4}$ cup orange juice
  Butter or cooking spray for the baking sheet

🕐 Prep time: 60 minutes
🕐 Baking time: 50–60 minutes
➤ Calories/cookie: About 195

1 | Preheat the oven to 350°F. Grease a baking sheet. Heat the honey, butter, and sugar. Mix all remaining ingredients with the honey mixture into a dough. Roll out half the dough onto the baking sheet and pierce numerous times with a fork.

2 | For the filling, purée the jam. In a bowl, combine jam, sugar, candied orange peel, almonds, and currants. Spread this mixture onto the rolled-out dough. Roll out remaining dough to the size of the baking sheet and carefully place on top of the filling. Press down lightly and pierce numerous times with a fork. Bake (middle rack) for 50–60 minutes.

3 | Make frosting with powdered sugar and orange juice. Spread it onto the hot cake. Cut the cooled cake into uniform squares.

Best When Fresh

Gingerbread

MAKES 60 COOKIES

➤ $\frac{1}{3}$ cup candied ginger
  $\frac{1}{3}$ cup honey
  $\frac{1}{2}$ cup butter
  $\frac{1}{2}$ cup sugar
  1 tsp vanilla extract
  2 eggs
  1 dash cinnamon
  $\frac{1}{2}$ tsp ground ginger
  1 dash pepper
  5 tbs orange juice
  1$\frac{2}{3}$ cups flour
  2 tsp baking powder
➤ For the frosting:
  1 egg white
  3 tbs lemon juice
  2 cups powdered sugar
  $\frac{1}{3}$ cup chopped candied orange peel
  Butter or cooking spray for the baking sheet

🕐 Prep time: 45 minutes
🕐 Baking time: 35–40 minutes
➤ Calories/cookie: About 60

1 | Preheat the oven to 350°F. Grease a baking sheet. Finely chop candied ginger. Heat the honey. Cream the butter, sugar, and vanilla. Stir in honey and all other ingredients. Spread batter onto the baking sheet and bake (middle rack) for 35–40 minutes.

2 | Beat egg white and lemon juice to soft-peak stage and drizzle in powdered sugar. Stir in candied lemon peel. Spread frosting on hot cake. Let dry out slightly and cut into diamonds.

Photo top: **Honey Cake Squares**   *Photo bottom:* **Gingerbread** ➤

Macaroon Batter— Delicate Seduction

No plate of Christmas cookies is complete without macaroons. They're the best way to go when you want something delicious and light—and when you're in a hurry!

53 Cappuccino Macaroons
53 Pistachio Macaroons
55 Hazelnut Macaroons
55 Coconut Kisses
55 Orange Macaroons

57 Chocolate Sesame Seed Macaroons
57 Poppy Seed Macaroons
57 Rosehip Macaroons
59 Anise Cookies
59 Cinnamon Stars

Quick Recipes

Cappuccino Macaroons

MAKES 50 COOKIES

➤ 3 egg whites | 1 tsp lemon juice |
²/₃ cup sugar | 4 tbs instant cappuccino
mix | ³/₄ cup ground almonds |
¹/₄ cup chocolate-covered coffee beans

1 | Preheat the oven to 325°F. Beat egg
whites and lemon juice until very stiff.
Drizzle in sugar while stirring constantly.
Sift in cappuccino mix and fold in almonds.

2 | Place the batter in a pastry bag with a
plain tip and pipe onto a baking sheet in
walnut-sized mounds about 2–3 inches
apart. Top each mound with 1 chocolate-
covered coffee bean and bake in the oven
(middle rack) for 20–25 minutes.

Pistachio Macaroons

MAKES 50 COOKIES

➤ ³/₄ cup pistachios | 3 egg whites |
1 tsp lemon juice | ²/₃ cup sugar |
1 dash anise extract

1 | Preheat the oven to 325°F. Line a baking
sheet with parchment paper. Finely grind
¹/₃ cup pistachios. Beat egg whites and
lemon juice until very stiff. Drizzle
in sugar while stirring constantly. Fold
in ground pistachios and anise.

2 | Place the batter in a pastry bag with a
large star tip and pipe small mounds onto
the baking sheet. Top each mound with
1 pistachio and bake in the oven (middle
rack) for 20–25 minutes.

Traditional | Easy

Hazelnut Macaroons

MAKES 50 COOKIES

➤ 3 egg whites
1 tsp lemon juice
$2/3$ cup sugar
$2\frac{1}{4}$ cups ground hazelnuts
$1/2$ tsp cinnamon
50 hazelnuts

🕐 Prep time: 40 minutes
🕐 Baking time: 20–25 minutes
➤ Calories/cookie: About 50

1 | Preheat the oven to 325°F. Beat egg whites and lemon juice until very stiff. Drizzle in sugar and continue beating until glossy. Loosely fold in ground hazelnuts and cinnamon.

2 | Place the batter in a pastry bag with a star tip and pipe onto a baking sheet in walnut-sized mounds. Top each mound with a hazelnut and bake in the oven (middle rack) for 20–25 minutes.

Crunchy | Easy

Coconut Kisses

MAKES 50 COOKIES

➤ **For the dough:**
1 cup flour
$1/3$ cup sugar
$1/4$ cup softened butter
1 egg yolk
➤ **For the macaroon batter:**
3 egg whites
1 tsp lemon juice
$2/3$ cup sugar
$2\frac{1}{4}$ cups grated coconut

🕐 Prep time: 1 hour
🕐 Baking time: 20–25 minutes
➤ Calories/cookie: About 55

1 | Mix the flour, sugar, butter, and egg yolk to form a dough, wrap, and refrigerate for 2 hours.

2 | Roll out dough to $1/8$-inch thickness. Cut out round cookies and transfer to a baking sheet.

3 | Preheat the oven to 325°F. Beat egg whites and lemon juice until very stiff. Drizzle in sugar. Fold in grated coconut. Place batter in a pastry bag with a large star tip and pipe small mounds onto the baking sheet. Bake (middle rack) for 20–25 minutes.

Fruity | Fast

Orange Macaroons

MAKES 50 COOKIES

➤ 3 egg whites
1 tsp lemon juice
1 tbs orange juice
$2/3$ cup sugar
Grated zest from $1/2$ orange
$1/4$ cup chopped candied orange peel
2 tbs grated chocolate
$1/3$ cup chopped almonds

🕐 Prep time: 40 minutes
🕐 Baking time: 20–25 minutes
➤ Calories/cookie: About 30

1 | Preheat the oven to 325°F. Line a baking sheet with parchment paper. Beat egg whites and lemon juice until stiff. Add orange juice and drizzle in sugar. Continue beating until glossy. Loosely fold in orange zest, candied orange peel, grated chocolate, and almonds.

2 | Place 2 teaspoon-sized small mounds on baking sheet, and bake (middle rack) for 20–25 minutes.

Easy

Chocolate Sesame Seed Macaroons

MAKES 50 COOKIES

- ➤ 1/3 cup semisweet chocolate, grated
- 1 1/2 cups sesame seeds
- 3 egg whites
- 1 tsp lemon juice
- 2/3 cup sugar
- 1/2 tsp cinnamon
- ➤ For decoration:
  2/3 cup semisweet chocolate or couverture

- 🕐 Prep time: 40 minutes
- ➤ Baking time: 20–25 minutes
- ➤ Calories/cookie: About 60

1 | In an ungreased pan, toast the sesame seeds. Preheat oven to 325°F.

2 | Beat egg whites and lemon juice until stiff. Drizzle in sugar. Loosely fold in sesame seeds, grated chocolate, and cinnamon. Place 2-teaspoon sized mounds on a sheet. Bake (middle rack) for 20–25 minutes.

3 | Dip the underside of each into melted chocolate; let harden.

Aromatic

Poppy Seed Macaroons

MAKES 40 COOKIES

- ➤ 3/4 cup poppy seeds
- 4 egg whites
- 1 tsp lemon juice
- 2/3 cup sugar
- 1 cup ground hazelnuts
- 1/2 tsp cinnamon
- 2 dashes cardamom
- 3/4 cup semisweet chocolate or couverture
- 2/3 cup plum butter
- 1 tsp rum (optional)

- 🕐 Prep time: 50 minutes
- ➤ Calories/cookie: About 80

1 | Preheat oven to 325°F. Grind poppy seeds. Beat egg whites and lemon juice until very stiff. Drizzle in sugar. Fold in poppy seeds, hazelnuts, cinnamon, and cardamom. Place batter in pastry bag with plain tip and pipe small mounds onto baking sheet. Bake (middle rack) for 20–25 minutes.

2 | Stir plum butter and rum until smooth. Spread this mixture onto the bottoms of half the macaroons. Sandwich together with remaining macaroons. Dip them halfway into melted chocolate and let harden thoroughly.

Traditional | Easy

Rosehip Macaroons

MAKES 50 COOKIES

- ➤ 3 egg whites
- 1 tsp lemon juice
- 2/3 cup sugar
- 1/2 tsp vanilla extract
- 3 tbs rosehip pulp (health food stores)
- 2 1/4 cups ground almonds

- 🕐 Prep time: 50 minutes
- 🕐 Baking time: 20–25 minutes
- ➤ Calories/cookie: About 50

1 | Beat egg whites and lemon juice until stiff. Drizzle in sugar and vanilla. Set aside 2–3 tbs stiff egg whites. Stir in rosehip pulp and loosely fold in almonds.

2 | Place the batter in a pastry bag with a large plain tip and pipe small mounds onto a baking sheet. Use handle of a wooden spoon to make a depression in the center of each and fill with a little stiff egg white. Refrigerate on the baking sheet for 2 hours.

3 | Preheat oven to 325°F. Bake (middle rack) for 20–25 minutes.

◀ *Photo top left:* **Chocolate Sesame Seed Macaroons**   *Photo top right:* **Poppy Seed Macaroons**
Photo bottom: **Rosehip Macaroons**

Traditional | Easy

Anise Cookies

MAKES 60 COOKIES

➤ **2 eggs**
  1³/₄ cups powdered sugar
  1¹/₄ cups flour
  ¹/₃ cup cornstarch
  2 tsp ground anise

🕐 Prep time: 40 minutes
🕐 Standing time: 12 hours
🕐 Baking time: 15–20 minutes
➤ Calories/cookie: About 30

1 | Beat eggs and powdered sugar until very creamy. Gradually stir in flour mixed with cornstarch and anise. Line a baking sheet with parchment paper.

2 | Make 2-teaspoon-sized mounds of batter with a 1-inch diameter on the baking sheet, placing them 1 inch apart. Let dry in a warm place for 12 hours.

3 | Preheat the oven to 325°F. Bake cookies in the oven (middle rack) for 15–20 minutes.

➤ Variation:

Spice Macaroons
Preheat the oven to 325°F. To make 50 macaroons, beat 3 egg whites and 1 tsp lemon juice until very stiff. Drizzle in ²/₃ cup sugar. Loosely fold 1³/₄ cups ground almonds, ¹/₂ tsp cinnamon, 1 pinch cloves, 1 pinch coriander, 1 pinch freshly grated nutmeg, and ¹/₄ cup chopped candied lemon peel into the stiff egg whites.

Place 2-teaspoon-sized mounds of batter onto a baking sheet lined with parchment paper. Bake Spice Macaroons in the oven (middle rack) for 20–25 minutes.

Traditional | Aromatic

Cinnamon Stars

MAKES 50 COOKIES

➤ **3 egg whites**
  1 tsp lemon juice
  1 cup brown sugar
  2¹/₄ cups ground almonds
  2 tsp cinnamon

🕐 Prep time: 50 minutes
🕐 Refrigeration time: 1 hour
🕐 Baking time: 15–20 minutes
➤ Calories/cookie: About 50

1 | Beat egg whites and lemon juice until very stiff. Drizzle in sugar and continue beating until glossy. Set aside 4 tbs for spreading on top later. Fold in almonds and cinnamon, and refrigerate mixture for 1 hour.

2 | Preheat the oven to 325°F. Place batter between 2 sheets of plastic wrap and roll out to ¹/₄-inch thickness. Cut out stars of various sizes and transfer to a baking sheet, placing them 2–3 inches apart. Spread with the stiff egg whites you set aside. Bake in the oven (middle rack) for 15–20 minutes. The stars should still be soft.

A

Almond(s)
cappuccino macaroons 53
chocolate sticks 33
Christmas bites 28
cinnamon stars 59
cookies 11
fruit squares 36
German gingersnaps 45
ginger bars 38
honey cake squares 50
honey rum cubes 48
lemon triangles 17
mocha triangles 38
orange macaroons 55
orange moons 21
orange tongues 35
rosehip macaroons 57
spiced stars 43
spice macaroons (variation) 59
sticks 26
Amaretto, poppy seed kisses 31
Anise
about 8
cookies 59
Apricot
Christmas bites 28
honey cake squares 50
honey rum cubes 48
tree cake cubes 41

C

Candied fruits (about) 8
Candied ginger
ginger bars 38
gingerbread 50
ginger hearts 17
Candied lemon peel
German gingersnaps
(lebkuchen) 45
spice macaroons (variation) 59
Swiss spice cookies 46
Candied orange peel
fruit squares 36
German gingersnaps
(lebkuchen) 45

gingerbread 50
honey cake bars 50
honey cake pinwheels 46
honey rum cubes 48
orange macaroons 55
spiced citrus cookies 45
Swiss spice cookies 46
Cappuccino macaroons 53
Cardamom (about) 8
Cashew sticks 19
Chocolate
coffee flowers 24
cresents (variation) 19
ginger bars 38
marzipan slices 24
mocha triangles 38
orange macaroons 55
sesame seed macaroons 57
squares 31
sticks 33
triangles 43
Cinnamon
about 8
stars 59
Cloves (about) 8
Cocoa
chocolate sticks 33
chocolate triangles 43
honey cake squares 50
orange moons 21
streusel hearts 21
three-tiered chocolate
cookies 21
Coconut
bars 23
kisses 55
Coffee
cappuccino macaroons 53
flowers 24
Cookie (see Dough)
Coriander (about) 8
Couverture
about 8–9
almond sticks 26

cashew sticks 19
chocolate crescents
(variation) 19
chocolate sesame seed
macaroons 57
chocolate sticks 33
Christmas bites 28
chocolate triangles 43
coconut bars 23
domino stones 48
eggnog S's 33
fruit squares 36
hazelnut corners 23
honey cake pinwheels 46
nougat rounds 13
orange tongues 35
pecan mounds 35
poppy seed macaroons 57
star sandwich cookies 28
tree cake cubes 41
troubleshooting 5
Currant jelly
almond sticks 26
domino stones 48
lemon triangles 17
streusel hearts 21
Currants
fruit squares 36
honey cake squares 50
squares 31

D

Decorating 7, 66
Dough
about 66–67
cookie (basic recipe) 4
cookie batter (basic recipe) 4
German gingersnap
(lebkuchen; basic recipe) 4
macraroon batter (basic
recipe) 4
tools 6
troubleshooting 5

E/F/G

Eggnog S's 33
Frosting
   decorating 7
   troubleshooting 5
Fruit squares 36
Ginger
   about 9
   bars 38
   hearts 17
Gingerbread 50

H

Hazelnut(s)
   bites 15
   chocolate squares 31
   chocolate triangles 43
   corners 23
   eggnog S's 33
   fruit squares 36
   German gingersnaps
      (lebkuchen) 45
   ginger hearts 17
   ginger bars 38
   Linzer cookies 17
   macaroons 55
   marzipan slices 24
   nougat rounds 13
   poppy seed macaroons 57
   sticks 33
   Swiss spice cookies 46
   three-tiered chocolate
      cookies 21
   vanilla crescents 19
Heidesand cookies 15
Honey
   cake pinwheels 46
   cake squares 50
   chocolate triangles 43
   domino stones 48
   German gingersnap
      (lebkuchen) 4
   gingerbread 50
   rum cubes 48
   Swiss spice cookies 46

L

Lemon triangles 17
Linzer cookies 17

M

Macadamia nuts, nut balls 11
Macaroon(s)
   batter (basic recipe) 4
   cappuccino 53
   chocolate sesame seed 57
   coconut kisses 55
   hazelnut 55
   orange 55
   poppy seed 57
   pistachio 53
   rosehip 57
   spice (variation) 59
Marzipan
   about 9
   domino stones 48
   heidesand cookies 15
   honey cake pinwheels 46
   orange wreaths 33
   pistachio pinwheels 26
   slices 24
Mocha triangles 38

N

Nougat
   chocolate sticks 33
   nut balls 11
   rounds 13
Nut(s)
   about 66
   balls 11
Nutmeg (about) 9

O

Orange
   honey cake squares 50
   macaroons 55
   marzipan wreaths 33
   moons 21
   tongues 35

P

Peanut bars 36
Pecan mounds 35

Pistachio(s)
   about 9
   macaroons 53
   pinwheels 26
Plum butter
   star sandwich cookies 28
   poppy seed macaroons 57
Poppy seed(s)
   about 9
   amaretto kisses 31
   macaroons 57

R

Raisins: honey cake
   pinwheels 46
Raspberry
   stars 13
   Linzer cookies 17
   three-tiered chocolate
      cookies 21
Rosehip macaroons 57

S

Sesame seed, chocolate
   macaroons 57
Spice(d)
   citrus cookies 45
   macaroons (variation) 59
Swiss cookies 46
Storing 67
Strawberry circles 13
Streusel hearts 21
Swiss spice cookies 46

T/V/W

Tools (see Dough)
Vanilla
   about 9
   crescents 19
Walnut rounds 15

ABBREVIATIONS

lb = pound
oz = ounce
tsp = teaspoon
tbs = tablespoon

The Author

Gina Greifenstein lives with her family in Germany. In addition to articles for newspapers, she also writes mysteries, children's books, and cookbooks. As a state-certified home economist, she learned cooking and kitchen crafts from the bottom up.

The Photographer

Jörn Rynio works as a photographer in Germany. His customers include national and international magazines, book publishers, and ad agencies. All the recipe photos in this book were produced in his studio with the energetic support of his food stylist, Petra Speckmann.

Photo Credits

P. 8–9: Teubner Foodfotografie
All others: Jörn Rynio

Published originally under the title Weihnachtsplätzchen: alle Jahre wieder © 2003 Gräfe und Unzer Verlag GmbH, Munich. English translation for the U.S. market © 2004 Silverback Books, Inc.

Program director: Doris Birk
Editors: Lisa M. Tooker, Randolph Mann, Stefanie Poziombka
Translator: Christie Tam
Readers: Bettina Bartz and Susanne Elbert
Layout, typography and cover design: Independent Medien Design, Munich
Typesetting: Patty Holden, Grafik Design Jürgen Bartz
Production: Patty Holden, Helmut Giersberg
Reproduction: reproteam siefert, Ulm

Printed in China
ISBN 1-930603-34-7

Enjoy Other Quick & Easy Books

Coffee and Espresso

Tanja Dusy

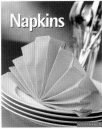

Napkins

1 Pan—50 Muffins

Fast Italian

Margit Proebst

Sauces and Dips

Irresistible Fondue

Angelika Illies

Cooking for Two

Cornelia Adam

Healthy Wok

Elisabeth Döpp
Christian Willrich
Jörn Rebbe

Great for light and satisfying meals

Antje Gruener

Grilling

Crisp, flavorful and full-of-flavor dishes straight from the grill for that barbecue flavor, from spareribs to skewered meats, garlic sauces and chutneys.

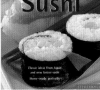

Andreas Fürtmayr

Sushi

Classic ideas from Japan and new fusion sushi
Home-made perfectly

Gina Greifenstein

1 Batter—50 Cakes

Baking to your heart's content

Cooking in Clay

Healthy Recipes with Great Flavor

Erika Casparek-Türkkan

1 Noodle, 50 Sauces

Everyday Pasta • Old and New Italian Dishes
Noodle biography • 10 Tips for Success

Doris Muliar

Cocktails for Drivers

100% Enjoyment

Antipasti and Tapas

Mediterranean Appetizers
Cornelia Schinharl

Soups

Classic to Contemporary

Sebastian Dickhaut

Claudia Schmidt

Raclette

New Recipes with Cheese Primer and Party Dips

Cornelia Schinharl

Easy Vegetarian

Uncomplicated and sophisticated –
Vegetarian recipes for all seasons

Cornelia Adam

Garlic

Sophisticated Recipes with this favorite spice of the Mediterranean. Flavorful, piquant (tangy). Pure delicacy, international

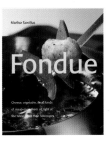

Marlisa Szwillus

Fondue

Cheese, vegetable, & all kinds of meat–cook them all right at the table. More fun than a recipe.

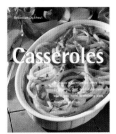

Sebastian Dickhaut

Casseroles

Delicious casseroles—right out of the oven, that special occasion dish. You need something new, flavorful and fun.

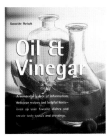

Annette Heisch

Oil & Vinegar

A wonderful source of information, delicious recipes and helpful hints—liven up your favorite dishes and create tasty sauces and dressings.

Cornelia Adam

Quiche

Delicious, tasty pies with vegetables, meat, poultry or fish—serve for all occasions

NUTS

- Ground hazelnuts and almonds quickly become rancid, so try not to keep them around for very long.
- Hazelnuts and almonds are easy to chop coarsely: Place them in a freezer bag and lay them on a hard surface. Then pound on them with a steak hammer until they've reached the desired consistency.

Guaranteed Perfect Christmas Cookies

BAKING COOKIES

- The best baking results are achieved when heat is radiated from above and below. With a convection oven, thin cookies quickly dry out.
- Line baking sheets with parchment paper so nothing sticks. You can reuse parchment paper several times.

DECORATED COOKIES

- Before putting away cookies coated with a glaze or chocolate frosting, be sure to let them harden thoroughly on parchment paper.
- Put parchment paper between layers of filled or frosted cookies so they won't stick together.

BAKING SHEETS

- Cookie baking goes much faster if you use more than one baking sheet. While one sheet is in the oven, you can already be loading the next.
- When it's time to bake your cookies, always transfer the cut dough to a cool baking sheet they'll keep their shape and won't spread out